OUR WARTIME LOVE STORY

IN MEMORY OF ANN ROGAN

BY

COLONEL JOHN F. ROGAN

US ARMY, RETIRED

Published by
Henschel HAUS Publishing, Inc.
www.henschelHAUSbooks.com

ISBN: 978159598-628-3 (Softcover)
ISBN: 978159598-629-0 (Hardcover)

Dedicated to the memory of my beloved wife, Ann.

TABLE OF CONTENTS

PREFACE

Writing this *Wartime Love Story* has been a labor of love for my father, John Francis Rogan. My parents were married for nearly 65 years until my mother's passing in 2015. It was wonderful to witness their deep and lasting love for each other as they raised nine children and moved from military base to base around the country and world. What a unique life we had!

My father understands that my mother's support on the home front was critical to his career success. He misses her dearly, as do all her children. This book represents his tribute to the wonderful wife and mother she was. I will always treasure the time that Dad and I spent together as we edited his narrative, selected family photos, and compiled the final manuscript.

With love and gratitude,
Patty Rogan

PROLOGUE

I am writing this story in memory of my beloved wife, Ann. I recently read the book *Dearest ones: A true wartime love story*, written by Rosemary Norwalk. She worked for the Red Cross Clubmobile in England during the war. The book was about the letters she sent home to her parents during that period, and she always addressed her letters "Dearest Ones" instead of "Dear Mom and Dad." I enjoyed reading this book, and others who also read the book said the story is very similar to the way I met my wife during the war. They suggested that I write my wartime love story. I hope you find it interesting.

—Colonel John F. Rogan, US Army, Retired

CHAPTER 1
MY LIFE PRIOR TO THE WAR

I was born on July 10, 1926 in New York City, the oldest of seven children in an Irish Catholic family. After the birth of my sisters, Millicent, Eileen, and Mary, my parents, John and Susan O'Doherty Rogan, decided to return to Ireland. We lived near my mother's home in Gortgarn, Northern Ireland, not far from Belfast, and I attended the same one-room Christian Brothers School that my mother had attended, and with the same school master, Mr. Gillespie. We also spent time with my father's family in Ballina, County Mayo.

My dad and mom met in Belfast. Dad was a police officer and my mother worked in a dressmaker shop. When my mother followed her older sister to New York City, it didn't take long for Dad to catch the next ship to New York, where they were married. I am not sure why they had returned to Ireland, but perhaps they were concerned about their mothers' health.

After approximately three years in Ireland, my father returned to New York, but my mother did not accompany him until he secured a job. After a short stint as a bus driver, Dad took a job in Elmira, New York, as a prison guard. Since he had been a police officer in Ireland, working at the prison seemed to be a good spot for him. Soon thereafter, my mother and the four children (Millicent, Eileen, Mary, and me) took a boat to New York and settled in Elmira.

Jack as a baby and young boy in Elmira, NY

Jack as a young boy in Elmira, NY

I attended Saint Patrick's parochial school and graduated with honors from Elmira Catholic High School in June 1944. I was very involved in basketball, football, and baseball. My biggest goal at that time was to become a professional baseball player—preferably with the New York Yankees. My mother, of course, was determined that her oldest son in an Irish Catholic family would become a priest, so she was not too keen about allowing me to enlist in the service. I was torn about pleasing my mother and at the same time, felt I should do my part by getting into the service.

John Rogan with sons Eddie and Jack Jr.

John Sr. in Reformatory uniform

Jack's mother, Susan

Jack's father, John

The Rogan home in Elmira, New York

From left: Mary, Eileen, Millicent, Susan (mother). In front: Joe and Tom

I decided to attend St. Andrews Seminary in Rochester, NY, but after one year, chose to relinquish my divinity status deferment and enter military service. I enjoyed my year at the Seminary but was not sure that I was called to be a priest. I felt compelled to serve my country. I also worried about what people would say if I left the seminary after the war ended.

I was inducted into the Army on June 29, 1945 at Syracuse, NY, and sent to Fort Dix, NJ for processing and testing before proceeding to Camp Wheeler, GA, for 17 weeks of combat infantry training. Since I was deemed qualified to attend Infantry Officer Candidate School upon completion of my combat training, I was also made a Squad Leader and was responsible for the performance of my squad members, as well as my own.

I will always remember the heat and humidity at that time of the year and the intensity of our training as we prepared for a possible all out invasion of Japan if the Japanese refused to surrender. Fortunately, my life was spared when the A-Bomb forced the Japanese to surrender.

Jack in high school, (1940-1944)

*Jack Rogan at St. Andrew's Seminary,
Rochester, New York (1944-1945)*

Consequently, instead of going on to OCS at Fort Benning, GA, I was transferred to the Finance Branch of the Army for necessary schooling at the Army Finance School, Fort Harrison, IN. After attending a few basic short-term classes, I was assigned briefly to the Finance Disbursing Office at Fort Logan, CO.

The major in charge of the office recognized my potential for further success and arranged for me to return to Fort Harrison for further training.

*Jack as a private at
Ft. Logan, CO (1946)*

Not long afterwards, I was assigned to the school faculty and was made an acting sergeant to teach enlisted personnel of various ranks. Eventually, I was persuaded to attend Finance Officer Candidate School for 17 weeks, graduating first in my class on November 1, 1946, and assigned back to the faculty as a young 2nd Lieutenant to teach commissioned officer classes. About that time, the Air Force became a separate branch of the service and began sending their former pilots, navigators, and others to these classes. It was certainly quite an experience for me as a young officer, but I soon became comfortable and capable in this capacity.

Jack as a Second Lieutenant in St. Louis, November 1946

Jack on the Ft. Harrison baseball team (middle row, second from right), 1945-1946

I should mention that I met my very first girlfriend, Margy Jones, when I first arrived at Fort Harrison for classes at the Army Finance School and she would often drive over to the school to see me when I had some free time. On weekends, I would be invited to her home in Indianapolis to hang out, watch TV, enjoy her grandmother's homemade cookies, and taking walks or drives around town. Unfortunately, it became much more difficult to keep in touch with Margery while I was attending Finance OCS due to the demands of the program and restrictions.

Our relationship became even worse when, shortly before graduation. the Army decided to relocate and centralize all finance functions at the former Ammunition Depot in St. Louis at Goodfellow and Natural Bridge. I managed to visit Margy over a weekend following my graduation and commissioning on November 1st, 1946, before continuing by train to Elmira to visit my parents and siblings while on leave.

Margy wrote to me every day while I was home and my dear mother took note of these scented letters. Eventually, we began to lose contact with each other as I became more involved in my new duties on the school faculty and with all the enjoyable things to do in St. Louis, such as attending the great World Champion Cardinal's games, taking up dancing lessons at Arthur Murray's studio, and beginning to date other girls, but not seriously.

Although I loved St. Louis and my faculty assignment and might have been able to serve my remaining time on active duty there, I finally decided to apply for a regular Army commission which, at my young age, involved being on a special competitive overseas assignment for one year as Deputy Finance Disbursing Officer at Camp Zama, Japan, near Yokohama and Tokyo. To be perfectly honest, I hated leaving St. Louis for my very first overseas assignment in a strange environment. Also, when I informed my parents of my decision, they were disappointed and worried that I had chosen a military rather than a civilian career back home.

In November 1948, I was transferred to Japan and assigned to the 198th Finance Disbursing Section in the Tokyo-Yokohama area. That was quite a transition for me, going from St Louis to an unknown situation in Japan. Some of the guys heard I had done some bowling in the past and talked me into joining a bowling team. Suddenly, we began to do very well and qualified to participate in the U.S. Army bowling championships in Kyoto in February 1949.

One of the Red Cross gals at Camp Zama heard that I was heading to Kyoto and said she had a friend there—Ann Cogan. She asked me to give Annr a call when I got there. Little did I know I was about to meet the "love of my life."

Ann Cogan in high school (1938-1941)

Ann Cogan, Cleveland, OH (about 1946)

CHAPTER 2
ANN'S LIFE PRIOR TO JAPAN

Ann grew up in Cleveland, Ohio. She was the oldest of seven children in an Irish Catholic family. Ann attended parochial schools and graduated from Lakewood High School in 1941.

After high school, she took a secretarial course and wound up in the typing pool in the sales division of the Standard Oil Company. Mr. Packard, who was head of the sales division, recognized Ann and her abilities and hired her to be his personal secretary. He was an avid Cleveland Indians fan and enjoyed studying Abe Lincoln, so he spent time skipping out to watch games and investigating Lincoln. Ann was responsible for typing up his notes regarding Lincoln.

After a while, she got a bit tired of the daily commuting. She was in a car pooling with guys who smoked cigarettes (and she was not a smoker). Ann felt she wanted to do something for the war effort and to do some traveling. She came across a Red Cross ad for people to serve overseas, so she checked it out and wound up in Washington for an orientation program.

Ann hoped she would be assigned to Europe, but wound up being sent to South Korea, where things were somewhat harsh in and around Seoul. Ann lived in a Quonset hut and rode around in jeeps. Eventually, she moved into a woman's billet in Seoul, but was then transferred to beautiful Kyoto, Japan, which had been untouched by the war. Ann was assigned to the Red Cross field office at I-Corps headquarters, which was also the location of the 25th Infantry Division. There were plenty of issues that demanded Red Cross attention.

I should mention at this point that, following the hiring and orientation procedures at the American Red Cross Headquarters in DC, Ann traveled by train to San Francisco, where she boarded the US Army transport *Republic*, a large troop ship, on her trip to the Korea. Fortunately, she and the other nine Red Cross women were first-class passengers assigned to staterooms on "B" Deck, which was the second from the top. The only other women on that deck were three nurses, four stewardesses, and two civilian women. In addition, a thousand young Army troops were on board, plus nine officers. The troops were not allowed on her deck and they could not mix or talk to the nurses. Since Ann had a lot of time on her hands during the trip, she volunteered to do typing for the Transport Surgeon.

In a letter home to her family during the trip, she mentioned enjoying free movies every night, but had to be in bed by eleven and up by eight each day. She did not get seasick at all and mentioned really enjoying the voyage.

Ann in Seoul, Korea (1948)

In contrast, I arrived by plane from St. Louis to San Francisco just in time to be assigned to a rather small ship at Fort Mason called the *Howard E. Woodford*, which was ready to sail to the Far East. In addition to the thirty to fifty of us on board, the only other cargo was a number of vehicles chained together below deck for delivery to military families in Japan.

Since we were leaving on the weekend, we had to settle for C-Rations instead of a decent meal as we passed under the Golden Gate Bridge and headed out to sea in a very turbulent ocean. We all became seasick—and homesick—that first night as we tried to cope with our duffel bags flying back and forth in our sleeping area, as well as trying to eat our meals with everything sliding back and forth across the mess tables. I often had difficulty sleeping as I listened to the creaking noises while the ship battled the turbulent and stormy ocean. We were seldom able to go up on deck for fear of falling overboard. There was a small PX in the area where all the cars were chained together, but it was only open for a short time each day during our trip and you had to be very careful about possible injury as well.

Ann prior to joining the Red Cross

Ann Cogan playing tennis with an army chaplain in Seoul, Korea (1948)

CHAPTER 3
JAPAN AND OUR BRIEF COURTSHIP

When I finally arrived in Japan in December 1948, after spending a few weeks crossing the Pacific on the US Army transport ship, named the *Howard E. Woodford*, we were bussed from Yokohama to Camp Zama, which had been the former Japanese military academy, like our West Point.

We soon became aware of the "honey bucket" odor from using human fertilizer on the crops, the occasional slight quakes, and the variety of older structures on the base. Camp Zama was primarily used as a processing center for military personnel arriving in the theater for subsequent assignment elsewhere.

When I stopped at the 198th Finance Disbursing Office, I was surprised to receive a warm welcome from Major Owen Boorom, whom I had met back in St. Louis. He informed me that I would be spending my one-year "Competitive Tour" as his deputy, which turned out to be a great assignment. He was a very fine mentor and became a lifetime friend afterwards.

Things were bleak during the winter weather at Zama, which made it difficult to leave the base. Thus, I joined the bowling team and began dating another Margy, a very nice USO person, and we enjoyed going to the movies and dancing at the Officer's Club. During nice weather, I would catch a ride into Yokohama or Tokyo with Major Boorom or our chaplain, Father Dennis Murphy, to have dinner and enjoy dancing at the Grand Hotel.

Much to my surprise, our bowling team managed to qualify for participation in the 8th Army Bowling Tournament to take place in Kyoto, Japan, beginning on February 9th, 1949. As noted above, a woman from the Red Cross mentioned knowing another Red Cross person, Ann Cogan, in Kyoto and asked that I give her a call upon arrival there that evening.

I contacted Ann right away and she invited me to their weekend party at the Ozawa House, where the Red Cross and Army Service Club women were billeted.

Upon arrival, I was immediately captivated by her beauty, grace, and charming personality. She resembled Kathryn Hepburn and Ingrid Bergman and fixed me my very first martini.

We spent most of the evening getting to know each other and discovering how much we had in common—similar last names (Cogan and Rogan), both Irish, and the oldest of seven in our Catholic families. Both of us had attended parochial schools, and Ann even considered becoming a nun before deciding to contribute to the war effort by working for the American Red Cross overseas.

As mentioned earlier, Ann hoped to be assigned to Europe, but was initially sent to the Red Cross Field Office in Seoul, Korea, the location of the 7th Infantry Division, for a year or so before being transferred to the Red Cross Field

Ann Cogan at American Red Cross field office, I Corps Headquarters, Kyoto, Japan (1950)

Office in Kyoto, Japan. That was the location of I Corps Headquarters and the 25th Infantry Division.

Fortunately, once we finally met in Kyoto in February 1949, we soon realized that we were meant to be together and began planning to marry in Lakewood, Ohio,

Jack Rogan and Ann Cogan soon after they first met (1950)

Visiting Nagasaki (1950)

On weekends, I would take the Friday night train to Kyoto, arriving at 6 a.m. Saturday morning. Ann would be waiting for me and we would spend the weekend playing tennis, swimming, or dancing at the Officer's Club, or traveling around the area in the car Ann had purchased in Japan.

I stayed in the BOQ on Saturday nights before heading back to Tokyo on Sunday evening in time to be at my office by 8 a.m. Monday morning. When Major Boorom realized how serious our relationship was becoming, he and his wife invited Ann to spend a weekend at their quarters at Camp Zama. Ann gladly accepted the invitation and the Booroms quickly agreed with our decision to be married.

Unfortunately, our plans to marry upon our return to the States had to be canceled when the Korean War suddenly began in June 1950 and we were all kept on indefinitely.

Since I was eventually approved for a regular Army commission, which also required serving two years with a combat branch, there was a good possibility that I could have been sent directly to Korea. Fortunately, my Finance Corps superiors at 8th Army Headquarters in Tokyo decided to keep me in Japan because I had been there since 1948.

In the meantime, Ann and I decided to apply for permission to marry as soon as possible in Kyoto. Thankfully, both applications were quickly approved and Ann used her connections at I Corps Headquarters to arrange for our marriage by a Catholic priest in the Post Chapel on July16, 1950.

Jack and Ann during their courtship in Japan

CHAPTER 4
SASEBO AND STARTING OUR FAMILY

We managed to enjoy a 24-hour honeymoon at the lovely Miyako Hotel before I was assigned to Sasebo as the Area Finance Disbursing Officer with responsibility for making necessary payments to the thousands of troops either processing through or returning from Korea as rotatees or wounded evacuees. Fortunately, Ann received Red Cross approval to join me in Sasebo since all the troops previously in Kyoto had been sent to Korea.

When I had first arrived in Sasebo, I was quite surprised to find that I recognized the Post Commander. I remembered meeting Col. Singleton previously when he stopped by our office at Camp Zama about a pay matter and I was able to resolve the problem for him. He couldn't have been nicer.

Because of the threat of an air raid from North Korea, dependents had been sent home for security reasons and there were lots of quarters available. The commander said that I should have Ann come down until and unless things got too dangerous. Thus, Ann and I had our pick of quarters and soon moved into in a high-rise overlooking the harbor where we could look out and see the 7th fleet coming into the harbor. Not surprisingly, we could not help but think about the Pearl Harbor attack in Hawaii.

I can't believe the pace we kept in Sasebo. I operated the downtown finance office during regular business hours, then in the evening, I went to Camp Mower to work all night processing thousands of troops, which required very close coordination with the Depot Commander, Post Commander, Rail Commander, and others. I was just a First Lieutenant working with colonels, but my being the area Finance Officer, they all needed to keep me in the loop.

I was also responsible for working with the supply officers in the 7th fleet, making sure we removed all American money from the sailors and replaced it with either military payment certificates or Japanese yen to guard against counterfeiting and the black market. Ann was always out there with me because there was likely to be different types of emergencies the Red Cross had to look into. Sometimes we'd eat our dinner at 2 or 3 a.m. in the morning, then were right back at the main office the next morning.

While living in our apartment overlooking the harbor, I somehow managed to hurt my back at work and have experienced back problems on and off ever since. This was a major concern because I was the only Finance Officer in the area and had to work long hours between the downtown office and the nearby Camp Mower troop processing center. For at least several weeks, I was in constant pain and just getting out of bed and dressed for work was a major effort.

Ann had to help me roll out of bed onto the floor so that I could crawl over to the bathroom, where she would help me into the large tub to soak. She would then help me out of the tub and across the room to the bed to help me stand and get into my uniform.

To ease the pain and resulting muscle spasms, Ann arranged for a Japanese man to come to our apartment in the evenings to give me a massage. This provided some temporary relief, but by morning, my back would be stiff as a board again. Much of the time, I felt like my back was broken, but thankfully the pain gradually subsided. Also, there were times when we had to head for a safe place when the air raid sirens jolted us right out of bed.

Ann became pregnant and she was not allowed to continue to work for the Red Cross. Our first child, Suzanne Elizabeth, was born May 7, 1951. Sasebo had no capability to care for pregnant women, so a month before her due date, Ann had to travel two hours by train to the 118th Station Hospital in Fukuoka (Hakata), Japan, where wounded GIs coming back from Korea were recuperating. I traveled to the hospital on weekends to keep Ann company.

After Suzanne was born, we decided to move from the high-rise into a little cottage in the hills of Sasebo, surrounded by Japanese families. The locals would come down from the hills and gather around Suzie when she was outside in her playpen. They marveled at her curly, golden-blond hair and her blue eyes.

We were together for another 22 months in Sasebo before returning to the States in April 1952 after four years in Japan.

Our cottage in Sasebo

Suzanne in her playpen in Sasebo, Japan in May, 1951

Ann with Suzie, 1951

Ann with Suzie in front of our cottage in Sasebo

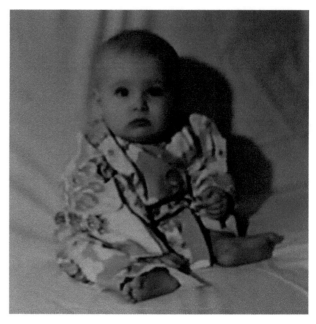

Baby Suzanne in a kimono (1951)

Jack, baby Suzanne, and Ann (1951)

Ann and Jack in Sasebo, Japan (1951)

CHAPTER 5
RETURN TO THE STATES

When leaving Sasebo, we had to take a train to Tokyo and then catch a prop flight to San Francisco via Hawaii and Wake Island. Needless to say, we didn't feel too perky upon arrival in San Francisco after taking turns holding Suzanne in our laps all the way back to the States. Nevertheless, we were excited about being back home and looked forward to spending the weekend in San Francisco.

The hotel where we were staying was very nice. I recall that there was a royal couple staying there and everyone at the hotel was dressed up. We arrived in the same clothes in which we had traveled and felt like crawling into the wall when we saw all the beautifully attired people in the lobby.

Suzanne was tired as well, so we decided to order room service. We couldn't believe the price of room service after the low prices in Japan! It didn't take us long to realize that we couldn't afford to stay there and we needed to head to Cleveland and then on to Elmira so Ann could meet my family.

It was an exciting time for us. We flew into Cleveland and the entire Cogan clan was there to meet us upon our arrival. Ann was so happy to see her siblings after being away for four years. I was delighted to meet her family, including her parents, Grace and James, and her siblings Lucille, Patty, Jim, Dick, Bob, and Gracie.

Ann drove me around the Lakewood area to show me the schools she attended, the Cedar Point amusement park, and where she had gone horseback riding and swimming.

Before leaving Cleveland, we had to purchase a car. Driving to Elmira, New York, scared us to death because people drove so fast. The speed limits in Japan were much slower. I was petrified driving our new car on the freeway, with people whizzing past us, and it took a while to get used to.

Ann with her siblings. From left: Ann, Lucille, Jim, Bob, Patty, and Gracie

Ann with her sisters, Gracie (on left), Lucille, and Patty

CHAPTER 6
FORT BLISS, TEXAS

It was time for me to get a new assignment. On the way to Elmira, New York, I received a telegram indicating that I needed to serve a two-year detail (1952-1954) with troops, and I needed to let them know right away what combat branch I wanted to spend the two years with—infantry, artillery, or armor. After 17 weeks of combat training at Camp Wheeler in Macon, Georgia, I wanted no part of going back into the infantry. I was too tall to be crawling in and out of tanks, so I decided to go into artillery.

Ann and I were not exactly happy campers when my orders to report to Fort Sheridan, Illinois, as Deputy Finance Officer, 5th Army Headquarters were canceled and I had to attend the Artillery Officer Course at Fort Bliss prior to being assigned to the 98th Battalion, 52nd Brigade at Fort Hancock, New Jersey, for my two years with troops.

At that time, highway and motel facilities left much to be desired during our long journey to El Paso. Many motels did not even have cribs, so Suzanne had to sleep with Ann or both of us. She was a very active child who slept very little in the car during the day. Also, as we approached the Texas border, we began to feel overwhelmed by the oppressive heat.

We finally arrived in El Paso in late afternoon the day before I was scheduled to report for schooling at Fort Bliss. Not having time to do any house hunting at that point, we decided to rent a brand-new, furnished efficiency apartment at a busy intersection called "Five Points," not far from the post.

Basically, the apartment consisted of one large open room with the living-dining area on one end and the bedroom on the other end, separated only by a bookshelf. We had a very small Pullman-type kitchen, which could be closed off by folding doors, and a nice bathroom. The living-dining area had vinyl furniture, as I recall, but we had no air conditioning! Even though it was only mid-May, it was already warm and getting more so each day. If we opened the window, we could hear the other tenants and they could hear Suzanne cry. Besides, it was too expensive to remain there.

Thankfully, we were soon able to move into a nice home the family was willing to rent for the summer while they were vacationing. The couple was also very nice and considerate and left everything in the house for our use, including their children's toys and swing. They also had a "swamp cooler," which used evaporation to keep the house nice and comfortable for the remainder of our time at Fort Bliss. It was also nice to be able to study in the evenings without disturbing Suzanne.

On weekends, we enjoyed going to the pool at the Officer's Club and sometimes Ann would take our infant there during the week. One day, Suzy stood up and began to walk when the pavement was too hot for crawling.

We also enjoyed having Ann's sisters, Patty and Gracie, visit us at Fort Bliss. We took them to Carlsbad Caverns one weekend, although they were mostly content to relax with Ann and Suzie around the house, and at the base pool.

Upon my graduation on August 29, 1952, we wasted no time escaping El Paso's heat and heading north for brief visits with our families before I had to report to Fort Hancock, New Jersey. We will always remember driving through a terrible dust storm that was so strong that dust managed to get inside the car even with the windows tightly closed. We were very concerned that the storm would damage the exterior finish of the car and made numerous "rest stops" along the way to check for damage and also to give Suzie a chance to get some exercise.

We managed to get a great picture of her standing on a picnic table at a fruit stop wearing only a diaper and munching on a large slice of watermelon. We were very thankful to have air conditioning in the car and not having any apparent damage from the dust storm.

Suzie on the road trip

CHAPTER 7
FORT HANCOCK, NEW JERSEY

My boss at Fort Hancock, New Jersey, was Battalion Commander Colonel Kelly, a fine West Point officer. It didn't take him long to realize I was a finance officer serving a two-year detail. He said he had enough battery commanders, so he would prefer to use me as his top assistant in charge of operations and training. He wanted me to ride along with him as he visited artillery sites around New Jersey. That turned out to be very interesting, but we'd be gone a good part of the day.

Back then, Ann and I found that everywhere we went, renting in New Jersey was expensive. Our first place was right outside the gate at Fort Hancock. One day, we woke up to find the area outside was flooded all around us between the river and the ocean. That wasn't a good thing, so we moved up north and ended up making four moves in two years.

I had to convince Colonel Kelly to give me something to command, so he let me take command of dog battery (D battery) in Newark, which was in really bad shape. Whatever I decided to do would be a big improvement.

Ann, Suzie, and I moved into a new high-rise, Ivy Hill Park Apartments, not too far from Branch Brook Park in Newark and close to Seton Hall University. We enjoyed living there and where we spent the last months of my two years with the combat arm.

I was anxious to return to the finance corps, although some artillery senior officers were trying to convince me to transfer to artillery because our "dog battery" (D battery) ended up being the best battery in the entire brigade.

Our family expanded when we had our second child, John Frances Jr. (nicknamed Jack) in Fort Monmouth, New Jersey, on March 23, 1953.

Jack Jr. with my parents, John and Susan Rogan

Jack and Suzie (1953)

Family photo in New Jersey (1953)

CHAPTER 8

CRANE AND FORT HARRISON, INDIANA, MY MASTER'S, AND A GROWING FAMILY

Upon completion of the two-year detail, I returned to the Army Finance School in Fort Harrison, Indiana, to attend the Advanced Officer Course from 1954 to 1955, and graduated #1 in my class. We lived at Fort Harrison from 1954 to 1958, but I didn't qualify for quarters on the base, so we lived in a duplex on North Wallace Street in Indianapolis. Then we moved into a house on North Audubon Road.

Kathy, Patty, and Colleen were all born at Fort Harrison between October 1954 and November 1958.

Jack and Ann received the "Loving Cup" for having the
most children during Jack's assignment at the Finance School

I was reassigned to the school faculty until 1958, when I was selected to attend graduate school at Indiana University in Bloomington, Indiana. I could have attended a university of my choice, but Ann and I decided I should go to IU, particularly because our family was growing larger and it would be a lot less expensive. We lived at the Crane Naval Ammunition Depot while I attended Indiana University from 1958 to 1960.

I had gotten to know the dean of the IU School of Business while I was teaching at the Finance School, so when I arrived on campus and met with the dean, we already had a friendship going. I had to be on campus during the summer before the MBA program began to meet residency requirements.

Ann with baby Kathleen, Suzanne, Jack, and Jack Jr. (1954)

Ann's mother, Grace Moriarty Cogan, with Kathy and Patty

Kathy and Patty in their scarfs

Kathy, Colleen, and Patty in matching outfits

We were able to obtain spacious quarters at the Navy Ammunition Depot at Crane, Indiana, which was about 45 minutes from Indiana University. We had access to the commissary and Post Exchange (PX), the Officer's Club, and other amenities at Crane. There were finance and other officers there who were also attending IU, so we took turns carpooling to and from campus. At the end of the week, we all got together at the Officer's Club to celebrate the completion of another week.

Ann was a huge support to me while I was completing my MBA school work. She would get up to type my papers in the wee hours of the morning, which made for a very long day for her after caring for our five children and being pregnant. I completed my bachelor's and MBA degrees between 1958 and 1960. Michael was born August 4, 1959—the night before a final exam.

Family with infant Michael (1959).

Suzie's First Communion, with Kathy, Jack, Ann, and Patty (1958)

While attending the MBA program, I was notified by the chief of personnel at the Pentagon that I was going to be assigned to Okinawa upon graduation from my master's program. We had time to make a short visit to our families in Cleveland and Elmira while we waited for our port call to go to Okinawa. As it turns out, we ended up staying with my parents in Elmira with our six children for what seemed to be an eternity and was stressful for my parents because our energetic children kept running up the front stairs and down the back stairs at their house.

Finally, I received my port call and we took a train to the West Coast for our flight to Okinawa. As you can imagine, it was quite an adventure for our children to be on a train and in a sleeper car. Ann and I took turns taking the children to the train's dining car for meals.

CHAPTER 9

OKINAWA

I was assigned to serve as the Deputy Director of Finance, U.S. Civil Administration, Ryukyu Islands, Naha, Okinawa, Japan, from March 1960 to June 1962. After a long and tiring flight to Okinawa, we arrived in Naha.

We were very excited about our new assignment, but encountered some unexpected problems upon our arrival. First, we were not met at the airport by my predecessor, Col. Harry Ford and his spouse, who we expected would act as our sponsors, welcoming us, taking us to our quarters, and making certain that everything was in order, such as enough groceries on hand until we were nicely settled in.

Instead, we were met by a single man who informed us that the Fords had received an early port call and had already left for the states. This person had no idea of what a sponsor's role should be and we were pretty much left on our own. We then discovered that our quarters had mistakenly been assigned to another family, so we had to spend a few days in temporary quarters until the problem was resolved. In addition, some of our children came down with measles and had to be quarantined for several days.

Fortunately, Col. Kriz, whom we knew from a previous assignment at the Army Finance School, heard that we had just arrived on the island and he and his wife, Hertha, quickly became our sponsors. We enjoyed getting together with them until they returned to the States.

To make things even more interesting, I had never been informed that I would not be wearing a uniform, except on formal occasions, during my USCAR assignment, so I had to have five suits made, in addition to a dress blue and dress white uniform for formal occasions at the Officers' Club with the High Commissioner. Ann also ordered a few dressy outfits to wear at these formal gatherings.

It also deserves mention that Colleen, who was only a few years old, caused us considerable concern when she came down with pneumonia soon after our arrival

Kathy, Jack, Ann with Mike on her lap, Suzie, Colleen, Patty, and Jack (1960)

and had to be hospitalized for several days. Thankfully, we did not encounter any other problems during our time on Okinawa and will always have fond memories of our time there.

We had a nice set of quarters in Naha, with two maids (Teriko and Chioko) and a gardener. The maids were a huge help to Ann, assisting with child care, cooking, cleaning, and laundry. We loved our neighbors and the kids made friends with the many children in the neighborhood.

My job was very fulfilling, with lots of responsibility for a young

In kimonos—Kathy, Patty, Colleen, and Mike (1960)

officer. I was a major then, but had moved into a full colonel's position. Thankfully, my direct supervisor, Brigadier General Ondrick, took a liking to me and gave me high ratings, which came in handy when being recommended for a promotion.

General Ondrick, who was the U.S. Civil Administrator, asked if I would take charge of arranging for the Annual St. Patrick's Day Dinner Dance, sponsored by the Okinawa Council of Catholic Men, to be held at each of the civilian clubs on the island as a fundraiser for Monsignor Felix Ley, the Apostolic Administrator of the Ryukyus, and his missionary group.

The day before the big dinner dance, I appeared on TV with Father Walsh, Chief Catholic Chaplain, for a 20-minute presentation about the role of the Okinawa Council of Catholic Men and plans for holding the Dinner Dance at the Harborview and Castle Terrace civilian clubs.

Thankfully, Joe O'Toole, a good Irishman and manager of the popular Harborview Club, agreed to assist in arranging for a very nice meal selection at both clubs for a very reasonable price of $5 per person, which covered dinner, four drinks, three floor shows, green hats, and much more. Our council also benefited from a percentage of the slot machine revenue that night.

Ann had to spend considerable time helping to solicit door prizes for the other club while Joe and I gathered door prizes for the dinner dance at Harborview, and printed the tickets, posters, and a souvenir menu. Ann and I were exhausted the evening of the dinner at Harborview where we sat at the head table with General and Mrs. Ondrick, honorary president of OCCM, and Msgr. Ley. Ann barely had time to dress for the occasion after spending most of the day gathering door prizes and having to depend on the maids to fix soup and sandwiches for our children.

Ann mentioned this OCCM involvement in a joint or combined letter to the Cogan and Rogan families on March 27th, 1961, when covering our activities on Okinawa to that point in time. She also mentioned her frustration about having one of our appliances after another needing repair due to the extreme heat, humidity, and rain on the island, which causes the current to fluctuate and everything metal to rust and corrode so fast. I was reminded about having to have our beautiful, new station wagon stripped down upon arrival and treated with a sealant to prevent corrosion. Thankfully, the procedure proved successful.

We enjoyed having plenty of time to doing things together as a family. We would go to the Ft. Buckner Officers' Club after Mass on Sundays. There was a separate area where the children could play and watch movies while Ann and I enjoyed a leisurely lunch together. We would also get in the car and drive around the island, including going to a rest center in Okuma at northern end of island and staying in a house there for three or four days.

We experienced several typhoons on Okinawa, which were severe rain storms with high winds. We would "batten down the hatches" by closing window shutters and propping up the furniture in our house, but the rain still seeped in and covered our floors. A foot of water flooded the streets after each typhoon.

A few of the houses in our neighborhood experienced roof damage from one of our strongest storms, which resulted in the placement of a heavy beam in the center of our living area as a protective measure. We hung Christmas cards and other wrappings on it to keep from bumping into it.

There were several occasions when the family and I were invited to a traditional Japanese tea house to enjoy a meal while sitting on cushions on the floor. We watched Geisha dancers and ate traditional Japanese food.

Ann in kimono

We were often invited to formal occasions at the Fort Buckner Officers' Club when the High Commissioner was entertaining the Ambassador or other distinguished guests. Because of the high temps and humidity, I would wait until arriving at the Club before putting on my dress uniform, or "Dress Mess." It was mandatory to be members of the club and our monthly billing included our prorated charge for that month's formal event.

The children attended schools run by the military, with some in Quonset huts. Jack and his friends created some excitement when they uncovered an unexploded artillery shell just across the street from our house that had been left over from the famous battle on Okinawa. Fortunately, the bomb disposal team arrived and took care of the shell before anyone was injured.

Jack, Jack Jr., and Kathy outside our house on Okinawa

In their Easter best: Suzie, Jack, Kathy, Patty, Colleen, and Mike

Kevin, our 7th child, was born October 12, 1961. It was so hot and humid that we had to run our two big air conditioning units virtually nonstop, and we had to keep a light on in the closets to prevent our shoes from molding. At night, Colleen liked to sleep up against the door of our bedroom so she could benefit from the cool air from our bedroom AC, but this may have caused her to get pneumonia.

President Eisenhower visited Naha while we were there and thousands of people lined up along the parade route to get a good look at the presidential caravan passing by. We were able to get a good view of him and his entourage as they passed our housing compound. It was the anniversary of Ernie Pyle's death from combat on April 18, 1945. A group of us from our USCAR Headquarters were able to chopper over to the small island of Lejima where Ernie, a much-loved war correspondent, had been killed. He is buried at the National Memorial Cemetery of the Pacific in Honolulu, Hawaii.

After two years in Okinawa, I was notified that I had been selected to attend the one-year regular course (1962-1963) at Command and General Staff College in Fort Leavenworth, Kansas. I was not too happy about this assignment because I was a finance officer and did not want to leave what I loved doing in Okinawa to spend a year fighting over offense and defense, and examining boring overlays. I also knew that I would receive another important finance corps assignment.

As we prepared to leave Okinawa, Ann decided to have the maids make matching outfits for the children to preclude the possibility of losing one of them during our layover in Hawaii on the long trip back to the States.

Leaving Okinawa (July 1962)

CHAPTER 10
FORT LEAVENWORTH, KANSAS

S uddenly we were back in the States at Fort Leavenworth, Kansas, with seven
children and no help for Ann. Our large family was assigned a large brick
duplex with a bomb shelter in the basement. Several other large families
were housed on our street, which made it fun for the children.

Ann with Kevin on her lap, Kathy, Jack, and Suzie in back row,
Michael, Patty, Colleen, and Jack in front row

As usually happened when we changed assignments, we arrived over the Fourth of July holiday weekend when it was scorching hot and humid and difficult to find stores open to purchase important items. Also, with her hands full keeping up with the move and our seven children, Ann had to rely on Suzanne and Jack to grocery shop on foot until we could purchase a new station wagon.

One day, I returned from class to find some of our children and their neighbor friends climbing up the back end of our new, red station wagon, walking across the roof in their cowboy boots, and sliding down the windshield. I was not very happy about the scratches, as I had opted to walk to class to prevent damage in the parking lot. However, on the bright side, there were lots of activities for our kids at Fort Leavenworth, and they enjoyed taking classes such as tap dance, ballet, and karate.

All things considered, our year at Fort Leavenworth's Command and General Staff College was relatively free of incidents, except for the scare Ann received on one occasion when Kevin, who

Kathy, Colleen, and Patty in front of our red station wagon

was only 9 months old at the time, managed to disappear from his playpen, which Ann had put on the lawn so he could watch the kids playing. At first, Ann thought that one of the older children had taken him out of the playpen, but began to panic when that was not the case. Fortunately, he was located before he might have been injured in some way.

Although the year was very busy and stressful, we survived it. Years later, when Ann and I had occasion to travel, we liked to stop at Fort Leavenworth to see what we had missed that year. It is a very nice post. Thankfully, near the end of the course, I was promoted to Lt. Colonel and assigned to the U.S. Military Academy at West Point, New York, which turned out to be a fantastic assignment.

Lt. Colonel Rogan (1963)

Jack being promoted to Lt. Colonel at the Command and General Staff College, Ft. Leavenworth, Kansas (1963)

Checking out our quarters was quite a project, especially with our large family. It involved a "white-glove inspection" of the entire house, including the stove, windows, walls, and floors. Consequently, most departing families opted for hiring special crews who were familiar with the strict inspection process and well worth the cost to avoid the hassle. Since I was still involved with class graduation, Ann did her usual great job of organizing all our belongings and dealing with the movers.

CHAPTER 11
WEST POINT, NEW YORK

At West Point, I served as Finance and Accounting Officer and Chief, Finance and Accounting Policy Division, Office of the Comptroller from 1963 to 1967. Since everything at West Point, such as quarters assignment and seating at athletic events and special performances, was based on your date of rank, we were assigned to a duplex on one end of the base until moving into a larger house on "Colonel's Road" overlooking the Cadet Chapel, and near the reservoir and Michie Stadium, where Army played football. Our white house stood out because of its wooden structure compared to the other brick homes on our street, but it was perfect for our growing family.

Lt. Colonel Jack and Ann at West Point, New York

Our parish, Holy Trinity, was just down the road from our quarters and our priests, Monsignor Moore and Father McCormick, were members of the Archdiocese of New York. I volunteered as a reader and usher at the Masses and Jack Jr. was a server at some of the masses. I also volunteered to assist Msgr. Moore in the fund-raising for the Cardinal Spellman Golden Jubilee, which took place in New York City during the Pope's visit.

For my assistance, Ann and I accompanied Msgr. Moore to the celebration at the Waldorf Hotel, followed by the Pope's masses at St. Patrick's Cathedral and Yankee Stadium. We always enjoyed the annual parish picnic as a family with lots of games for the children, great food, and a good opportunity for parents to get better acquainted with other parishioners.

Our children enjoyed being involved in many activities, including the swim team. All of the kids swam competitively year-round, beginning at a young age. Ann and the children spent many hours at Delafield Pond during the summer months; it had a sandy beach area, as well as platform and spring diving boards. The older children were able to attend "sleep away" camp in the summer.

We enjoyed attending the Army—Navy football games and observing the cadets engaged in their various activities, including marching on the parade grounds, struggling through the grueling "slide for life" endurance course, and marching back and forth near their dormitories as they served their demerits.

Jack Jr. had his heart set on becoming a cadet and loved watching the cadets from our screened porch overlooking the cadet barracks and parade ground. He kept his room immaculate and made his bed just like a cadet. He passed the physical exam with flying colors, but failed the medical exam due to a lower back problem. Needless to say, he was very disappointed. He would have been an outstanding cadet and future officer.

One day, we decided to visit the Bear Mountain Zoo, which was not far from West Point. Shortly after arriving we suddenly realized that Kevin, who was about four years old, was not with us. We began frantically searching for him, fearing that he might try climbing into a bear cage or the like. After notifying zoo personnel of his sudden disappearance, we decided to check the parking lot. Much to our relief and amazement, he had somehow managed to find his way back to our car and was very teary-eyed and relieved to see us—and vice versa.

Although it was difficult for Ann and me to get a break from our family responsibilities, we managed to attend dance lessons at the Officers' Club and occasional drives into New York City to catch a popular play and enjoy a nice dinner at a favorite restaurant.

Since it was important that I keep in good physical shape, I would often play volleyball or bowl with our team during the lunch hour. I also played in a fast-pitch softball league after work with Bobby Knight, the young head basketball coach who later became a coaching legend.

Soon after arriving at West Point, my brother Joe drove up from Elmira with my mom and dad for a weekend visit while we were still in duplex housing. Soon afterwards, we were also visited by my sister Millicent and family.

David and Maureen, our eighth and ninth children, were born during our time at West Point. We were very happy that Ann's sisters, Patty and Gracie, visited us from the Cleveland area and were of great assistance.

While we were at West Point, in addition to the Pope's visit, General MacArthur gave his famous speech to the Cadet Corps. Also during this time John F. Kennedy

Jack and Ann with all 9 children, including newborn Maureen (1965)

was assassinated, the World's Fair was held at Shea Stadium, the Beatles made their first appearance in New York, and General MacArthur died. What special memories we will always have from our four wonderful years at West Point.

After four years, the Chief of Personnel at the Pentagon informed me that it was time for me to go to Seoul, South Korea, for a 13½-month unaccompanied tour. I was to serve as a Finance and Accounting officer, and, during the second half of my tour, as Chief of the Finance and Accounting Policy Division, Office of the 8th Army Comptroller. This was especially difficult to accept because by then David and Maureen had been born at West Point, and Michael had been diagnosed with Huntington's chorea. Ann would be alone with our nine children for more than a year.

Family photo, including baby Maureen (1965)

Kevin, David, and Maureen (1965)

CHAPTER 12

CORNWALL, NEW YORK AND MY HARDSHIP TOUR IN SEOUL, SOUTH KOREA

It was very difficult for Ann and the children to have to leave our nice quarters at West Point after four wonderful years, but it was necessary since my assignment to Seoul, Korea was considered a "PCS" (permanent change of station). We decided to move to Cornwall, New York, because of its convenient location to West Point, where the children were still involved with swimming and other activities, and where Ann needed to shop at the commissary and PX. Our new house was quite small compared to our quarters at West Point, with up to three children in each bedroom and Jack Jr. in the basement.

In addition to having to change schools in the middle of the school year, and the inconvenience and very high rental charges for a much smaller house for that period that I would be away, we were very concerned about Ann having to

Summer fun with friends in Cornwall, New York. Pictured: Kevin, Patty, Maureen on Colleen's shoulder, and David (1967)

commute almost daily to West Point by driving on the winding Storm King Mountain roads which were often icy and dangerous in bad weather. At that time our station wagon did not have seat belts.

Besides having all nine children, including a toddler and an infant, to care for, another concern was Michael's health situation as mentioned in the last chapter. Thankfully, by strictly following the doctor's orders and making certain that he managed to get plenty of rest, Michael recovered nicely.

Mike, Kevin, David, and Maureen in Cornwall, NY

Doing gymnastics. Back row: Suzie, Patty, Colleen (with Maureen on her shoulders), and Jack. Front row: Colleen, Mike, Kevin, and David

In back from left: Jack, Patty, Maureen being held by Colleen, Mike, and Kathy. In front: David and Kevin

*David and Kevin after getting
into the black markers*

Before leaving West Point for Korea, I managed a brief visit to Elmira to visit my parents. They had visited us with my brother Joe when we first arrived at West Point and we had also made a few visits to Elmira during my time at the Point.

This visit was particularly sad and difficult because I knew that Dad was in the final stages of dementia and did not have much longer to live. He was confined to bed by that time and was unable to communicate with me even if he knew who I was. I had that terrible feeling that I probably would not see him again.

Dad passed away on July 17, 1967, the day after Ann's and my 17th anniversary. I took a military flight back from Korea to Elmira via West Point so that Ann and I could attend his funeral, visit my mother and siblings, and spend a few days with Ann and our children in Cornwall before returning to Korea. On the bright side, it made my last six months away seem a bit easier to take.

During my 13 months in Korea, Ann and I communicated by tape recorder or snail mail because it was prior to cell phones, e-mail, or Skype. I would make a tape recording every weekend and send photos of places I had visited. Ann would gather the children around the table to hear my recording before recording a response. Also, to pass the time, I took an

*My parents,
John and Susan Rogan*

Ann and the kids having Christmas dinner at the Officers' Club while I was in Korea

evening teaching position at the university and used the extra money to send gifts to Ann and the children.

Unfortunately, just prior to my return from Korea, there was a very heavy rainstorm in Cornwall. Our house was on the low end of the street and the drainage system got clogged with leaves, causing our yard to fill up with water like a pond. Water poured into our basement. The muddy, waist-high water ruined all our precious mementos from our time in Japan and Okinawa. Ann waded around in the water trying to salvage our belongings, including our son Jack's possessions. Although the firetrucks pumped water out of the basement all that night, there was still a muddy mess to welcome me home.

Ann shared more of the difficulties that she had encountered during my long absence. Our older children were tired of making so many moves, which meant leaving their friends and starting in new schools every few years. As much as I wanted to be a general, it was much more important to give the family top priority.

CHAPTER 13
BACK TO FORT BENJAMIN HARRISON

Although I had just been promoted to colonel in April 1968 and was on the fast track to general officer rank, it became very clear that our marriage and family should always have top priority. Accordingly, I notified my good friend Russ Chapin in Washington, D.C. of my intention to retire on June 30, 1970 upon completion of the two-year commitment to serve after accepting the promotion to colonel. He agreed with my request to serve my final two years at Fort Harrison as Director of Settlements Operations at the huge Army Finance Center.

I was quite surprised to find that there had been a recent change in command at the Finance Center, which caused some dissention among the senior staff and the large number of civilian employees. As it turned out, the new Commanding General (CG) had transferred from the Medical Services Branch as a brigadier general, bypassing the senior Finance Corps officers who were aspiring to become generals. The new CG was very tough and shook things up, but made necessary changes to improve the overall efficiency of the Center.

Although I was the youngest colonel on the staff, I was appointed Director of Settlements Operations, the largest Directorate, which encompassed four separate divisions with nearly 1300 employees. Each division was headed by a lieutenant colonel who reported to me and I also had a senior ranking civilian as my deputy. Since the other three directors were nearing retirement, the new CG and I got along pretty well and I was asked to chair his farewell party when he was appointed Chief of Finance and promoted to major general.

Needless to say, the family and I were all delighted to return to Fort Ben, which I had always considered "home," since my previous assignments had been there while attending OCS and serving on the staff and faculty at the Finance School. Also, as noted previously, Kathy, Patty, and Colleen were all born at Fort Harrison between 1964 and 1968.

It was wonderful to finally get very nice, large quarters at 660-B Lawton Road right along the parade grounds. In addition to the bedrooms and bath on the second floor, there were also two large bedrooms and a bath on the third floor, where four of our girls enjoyed the privacy.

The younger boys enjoyed playing around the large cannon on the edge of the parade grounds nearest our quarters. The children also enjoyed being on the post swim team and being able to swim at the Officers' Club pool as well.

Jack managed to get a job as a caddy at the golf course and could play a little golf when the course was not that busy. In addition to enjoying dinners and other

Quarters 660B Lawton Road, Fort Harrison, Indiana

social or "Hail & Farewell" events at the Officers' Club, Ann and I bowled in the married couple league and I also bowled in the men's league. I was a pitcher for the Finance Center team in the fast-pitch softball league.

We also enjoyed ice cream treats at nearby favorite places just outside the base on steamy evenings and weekends. A few times, we drove or took a post bus to watch the time trials at the Indiana Speedway track. When the weather was favorable, I would occasionally walk to the Finance Center past the old brick buildings along the parade grounds, where I used to attend classes in earlier time before joining the Finance School Faculty as an instructor.

A number of new facilities had been added since out previous assignment at Fort Ben, such as a new chapel where our baseball field used to be, and an attractive Finance-Adjutant General School Complex. Unfortunately, after also adding a new commissary, Post Exchange and large hospital complex, the Pentagon decided to close Fort Harrison as an active post sometime after my retirement on June 30, 1970.

Fortunately, the planners have done an excellent job of converting much of the old post into an attractive development with a large area being reserved for a state park. The spacious brick homes around the parade grounds, which were mostly occupied by generals and colonels, have since been completely renovated and placed on the market for sale. The good news is that the former Officers' Club and golf course remain open and the University of Indiana frequently holds faculty retreats there, which Patty, now a professor at UI, has attended.

Shortly before my retirement ceremony, we received a surprise and enjoyable visit from retired Colonel Owen Boorom, my former boss and mentor when I was assigned to the 198th Finance Disbursing Unit at Camp Zama, and his wife Ellen. Just prior to my formal retirement on the parade grounds, Colonel Clancy, the acting Finance Center Commander, presented us with a beautiful silver tray on behalf of the Finance officers at the Center and their wives.

Ann and Jack receive a silver tray on behalf of the
finance officers and their spouses

Thankfully, the weather was perfect for my retirement ceremony, which was well attended by family and friends. Six others of various ranks were also retiring that day. Navy Captain J. B. Smith handled the necessary introductions and Rear Admiral Lawrence Geis, Navy Chief of Information, pinned the Legion of Merit medal on my uniform and also presented me with Certificates of Appreciation from the President, Secretary of Defense, and the Chief of the Army Finance Corps in recognition of my 25 years of continuous active duty encompassing WWII, Korea, and

Vietnam. However, I did find it a bit unusual for Navy officers to participate at a retirement ceremony at an Army base.

As I stood at attention on the parade field on June 30, 1970 so many nice memories of Fort Harrison passed through my mind and nearly brought me to tears. In addition to recalling my days as a student in 1945, my OCS Commission in 1946, and faculty assignment until 1948, I recalled playing baseball for the Fort Harrison team on weekends against nearby Camp Atterbury and local teams within a fifty-mile radius of the base. Back then, a large number of German and Italian prisoners of war were housed at Fort Harrison and worked on various projects around the base.

I will always have a warm spot in my heart for Fort Ben and the people of Indianapolis and the state in general, who were so good to the military. Since our daughter Patty, who was born at Fort Ben along with Kathy and Colleen, is also a Professor of Education at Indiana University, which is also my alma mater, I take full advantage of every opportunity to revisit the city and Fort Ben.

My retirement ceremony on the parade grounds at Fort Harrison, June 30, 1970

CHAPTER 14
MADISON, WISCONSIN

After my retirement from the Army, I needed to give serious thought about what I wanted to do next. I spent a good amount of time looking into civilian job opportunities. With nine children, I could not just put my feet up and retire. I narrowed my search to two positions. One was in San Antonio, Texas, where other military personnel had retired. The position was the Vice President of Finance at St. Mary's University, but I was not too keen on the hot and humid weather there.

I came across an ad for the State Finance Director position in Madison, Wisconsin. Ann and I had never been to Wisconsin, but it seemed like something I should look into. I made a phone call to Governor Knowles, who asked me to come for an interview. The governor let me know about the many problems with the finance organization at the state. The position sounded like a real challenge due to all these problems. I felt that with my financial management background, I could help to straighten things up.

Since we had to relocate to Madison from Fort Harrison no later than June 30, 1970, the effective date of my retirement from the Army, I took leave from my position as Director of Settlements Operations at the Finance Center to find a suitable house for our large family in an area with easy access to schools, churches, shopping malls, and entertainment areas.

During working hours at the Wilson Street Office Building in Madison I kept very busy trying to get on top of my new State Finance Director duties and responsibilities. After work and on weekends, I spent time with a realtor checking out numerous homes large enough to accommodate our family and convenient to the University of Wisconsin. Fortunately, I was able to purchase our wonderful home on Boulder Lane here in Middleton in time for Ann and the children to move in over the July 4th weekend.

Prior to our move, Ann came to Madison with me one weekend in the winter to check out the city. It turned out to be a very cold weekend. We stayed at the Lorraine Hotel on the Capitol Square. Despite the freezing temperatures as we walked around the Square to the various stores, we decided to accept the position.

We were looking for a place to live in retirement that was not a huge city. Ann asked me not to accept a position in a big city, although that is where most of the highest-paying positions were located. I accepted the job with the assurance that as the State Finance Director, I would be independent of political ramifications. That is a good thing because I ended up working with five governors: Warren Knowles, Pat Lucy, Marty Schreiber, Tony Earl, and Lee Dreyfus.

Ann and children were delighted with our new home and location and made many new friends within a short time. There were quite a lot of young children in our neighborhood when we arrived who were quickly at our door to meet our children. It did not take long for our children to get involved with the Middleton swim team, high school sports, and other neighborhood activities. Ann and I soon became actively involved with our St. Bernard's Parish and the Madison Diocese and continued this involvement for many years until age and health-related problems intervened.

When we first arrived in Madison, there were anti-war protests and some violence taking place in Madison, including the bombing of Sterling Hall on the University campus, which resulted in the death of a research person, and the fire-bombing of the ROTC facilities. These were of concern, as was the sudden decision by the Defense Department to close Truax Air Base, where we hoped to be able to utilize their PX, commissary, and Officers' Club facilities.

Shortly after moving into our home on Boulder Lane here in Middleton, I received a call from Charlie Cheever at Saint Mary's University in San Antonio, hoping I would take the VP of Finance position there. I knew his father, who was president of US Automobile Association (USAA) at the time I was Director of Finance and Accounting at West Point. He had tried to persuade me to retire and take his job at USAA. However, our household goods had just arrived in Madison, so it was too late to make a change. Fortunately, things settled down and we fell in love with the Madison area and all that the city and state have to offer, such as the University campus and the beautiful surrounding lakes.

During my time as State Director of Finance, I became very involved in the National Association of State Auditors, Comptrollers, and Treasurers (NASACT) and

*Family photo in our Middleton home (1970). Seated on floor: Patty and Maureen.
Seated on chair: Colleen, Sue, Ann, and Jack.
In back: Kevin, Mike, Kathy, David, and Jack Jr.*

ultimately became the organization's president. This role involved periodically flying to Washington to work with federal officials on behalf of all fifty states.

Soon after arriving in Madison, I met Bishop O'Donnell, who had recently come from Chicago. We were both Irish and he had a good sense of humor. The next thing I knew, I was becoming very involved in Diocese activities, including serving as a member of the corporate board and other boards and committees, as well as serving a four-year term as a member of the US Catholic Bishop's Advisory Council. As it turned out, I volunteered my financial management expertise to three bishops—O'Donnell, Bullock, and Morlino—for more than 38 years until June 2008, when Ann's declining health situation required my full-time presence at home.

Our house at 6640 Boulder Lane in Middleton was perfect for our large family, although a bit cramped until the older ones finished high school and went off to college. The house is a tri-level with four bedrooms, den, two and a half baths, a living-dining area, kitchen, huge family room, and a three-quarter basement. We also have a large front and spacious backyard with about twenty huge, old oak trees to provide plenty of shade during the hot summer months. It was such a joy to finally have a home of our own after our many relocations during my 25-year active duty career in the Army.

In front of the fireplace at Christmas.

When Ann and I first took note of the nice flower garden just outside our front entrance and the orange/reddish color of our front door, we immediately felt the urge to add a Japanese-style waterfall and small bridge in the backyard off the patio for our enjoyment. However, we soon came to our senses when we realized how much the children loved playing in the yard with their friends.

Since most of the houses we had lived in during our many tours of duty contained government-owned furniture, it was necessary to purchase all new furniture for every room, including replacing the carpeting installed by the previous owner and, little by little, the major appliances as well.

Shortly after our arrival in Middleton, Kathy, Patty and Colleen decided to spend 17 days visiting their friends at Fort Harrison. They were able to swim in several meets on the swim team which they were on last summer, brought home some ribbons, and had a nice finish to their summer vacation. Jack Jr. took part in the Explorer Scout canoe trip to Canada, returning the day after school started.

Also, not long after our arrival, Maureen, who was only about five at the time, was seriously injured on her bike on busy University Avenue when she tried to follow some of the older children for an ice cream treat at dusk. I was just returning from the West Towne Mall and noticed the flashing lights of the ambulance as I turned onto University Avenue. I had no idea who had been injured until I pulled into our driveway a few minutes later. Maureen's femur bone had been broken, but, fortunately, she made a complete recovery after a lengthy hospital stay with her leg in traction. We will always be grateful to Doctor Heiden for taking such special care of Maureen at Madison General Hospital.

Most of our spring break trips were to Disneyland in Florida, which the children enjoyed. We would usually take our two cars in order to fit everyone. When we stopped along the way, some of the children were able to switch to the other car or to a different seat. Ann always did a remarkable job of planning for the trip and proper routes to follow. She always kept a notebook of our expenses along the way. David had a talent for drawing clever and hilarious sketches of our family, with captions, at restaurant stops and other interesting places along the way; we still enjoy perusing those at family gatherings.

On what would be our last spring break to Disneyland, Michael created a bit of a stir when he insisted that he would not go along unless his girlfriend Wendy could be with us. Fortunately, the problem was resolved when Wendy received permission to use her family's station wagon. We resembled an Army convoy with our three vehicles and had to pay close attention to the two vehicles following behind us for fear that we would lose them if they took a wrong turn or had a mechanical problem of some sort.

Eventually, the stress I was under due to my increasing responsibilities as State Finance Director, combined with my involvement with the National Association of State Auditors, Comptrollers and Treasurers (NASACT) as president, and many years of assisting the Diocese of Madison, began to take its toll on my blood pressure and overall health condition. Ann and my doctor were very concerned about the likelihood of having a serious stroke because I also had an irregular heartbeat.

Fortunately, I took the necessary and appropriate action to step down from my State Finance Director responsibilities in August 1983, when I also completed my term as President of NASACT. I continued to volunteer my services to the bishops of the Diocese until experiencing a minor stroke over the St. Patrick's Day weekend in 1996. Thankfully, I made a quick and complete recovery and could continue my assistance to the Diocese on a more limited time basis until it became necessary to step down from that role to become Ann's caretaker.

Dressed up for the Sax Woods annual neighborhood gathering

Ann visiting her family in Cleveland (1972)

After our children were grown and out of the house, Ann and I enjoyed driving to Colorado in September to visit our son Jack and his family in Grand Junction, stopping on the way in Colorado Springs to visit Irish cousins Paddy and Michael O'Doherty, whose homes at the time were right next to each other. Their fathers were my mother's brothers. Before returning to Madison, we also stopped for a short visit with our son Kevin, who was working in Colorado at the time.

From left: Colleen, Ann, and Kathy vacationing in Hawaii

Jack and Ann during one of their annual trips to San Diego in January

Following a NASACT conference in Texas, we were able to drive over to Houston to visit my sister Millicent and her lovely family. Another enjoyable car trip was to Fort Myers, Florida, to visit my sister Mary and husband, Myers Thurber, who had a high rise condo right on the beach where they would spend part of the winter season away from Elmira, New York.

When I was still on active duty in the military, Ann and I enjoyed driving to Florida and staying in VIP Quarters at the various Army and Air Force bases along the way to Panama City and other lovely places. We decided to make a similar trip from Madison for old times' sake, but encountered steady rain during our drive down the East Coast all the way to Miami. At that point, with showers still in the forecast, we decided to pass on Panama City and head directly to Key West instead, which we enjoyed on our first and only visit there.

Ann and I also volunteered our services in numerous capacities to our parish of St. Bernard's in Middleton for many years. I was Parish Council President and continued to volunteer my services as financial advisor, reader, and communion distributor. Ann was also a communion/wine distributor at the evening masses and volunteered to help with other fundraising or charitable activities, such as the annual rose sales and clothing drives.

On July 16, 2000, we celebrated our 50th anniversary with a wonderful mass at St. Bernard's, celebrated by our bishop, William Bullock. It was followed by a reception at Bishop's Bay Country Club, where hundreds of our relatives and friends joined our celebration. This included a luncheon, Irish music, and a video loop of family photos.

Our 50th wedding anniversary (2000)

Jack and Ann's 50th Wedding Anniversary
(Photo taken at St. Bernard's Catholic Church, 2000)

At Jack and Ann's 50th Wedding Anniversary. From left: Jack's brother Eddie, cousin
Eileen, Jack's brothers Joe and Tom, Ann, Jack, and Jack's sister, Millicent

Early on, Ann and I became members of the Equestrian Order of the Holy Sepulcher of Jerusalem, North Central Lieutenancy, where I also volunteered my services on the finance committee for several years. We were able to attend the annual meetings in the various states until Ann's health became a concern. One of our most enjoyable annual meetings took place at Notre Dame University in South Bend, Indiana, in the fall of 2007. Mass was held in their beautiful chapel and we were also able to watch the football team's home game.

Jack and Ann as members of the
Equestrian Order of the Holy Sepulcher
of Jerusalem (2007)

CHAPTER 15

BLESSINGS DURING OUR TIME
IN MADISON

In 1993, I was honored to be selected by the Veterans Administration for outstanding community achievements since leaving military service.

On Sunday afternoon on November 23, 1997, at Saint Raphael's Cathedral in Madison, I received the Papal Honor of "Knight Commander of Saint Gregory the Great" with two other great and deserving friends. Our longtime friend and pastor of our parish at the time, Msgr. Joseph Higgins, also received the "Prelate of Honor."

It was a beautiful ceremony in every respect with a huge turnout. Knowing in advance that we would be receiving these honors, Father "Pat" and I arranged for a special dinner celebration at our parish afterwards with our many friends. What a memorable occasion!

In June 2003, our family received both the State of Wisconsin and Diocese of Madison "Family of the Year" awards from the Wisconsin Knights of Columbus.

Photos taken after Jack received the Papal Honor of
"Knight Commander of Saint Gregory the Great" (1997)

Jack in the uniform of the "Knight Commander of Saint Gregory the Great" (drawn by son David, 1997)

From May 27 to June 3, 2004, we attended a most memorable Pilgrimage to Rome and Assisi with our bishop, other members of the Equestrian Order of the Holy Sepulcher of Jerusalem, and seminarians from our Diocese. The pilgrimage included the rosary in the Vatican Gardens, Mass at the various basilicas, an audience with the Pope, and a visit to Assisi. We managed to get a nice close-up photo of Pope John Paul II as he made the rounds in his "Pope mobile" in St. Peter's Square. We also received a great photo of our pilgrimage group, which we will always treasure along with the photo of the Pope. On September 30, 2004, Bishop Robert Morlino, our bishop, invited all of us to a Rome pilgrimage reunion gathering, which was very nice.

I was honored to be profiled in the "Know Your Madisonian" section of the *Wisconsin State Journal* on December 11, 2004. Also in 2004, after serving as the President of the Madison Club, I was honored to be named "Serran of the Year" in recognition of my service.

In February 2009, the Wisconsin Board of Veterans Affairs awarded me the "Veteran's Lifetime Achievement Award," for which I was most honored. It was also quite an honor to have our family featured in an article in the June 25, 2009 issue of the *Middleton Times Tribune*. The very nice article was titled "Jack Rogan: Living the Good Life," and included the story of how Ann and I met and married in Kyoto, Japan in July 1950.

John Rogan gets Veteran Lifetime Achievement Award

Wisconsin Board of Veterans Affairs
Veteran Lifetime Achievement Award

Past Award Recipient
February 2009
(presented April 2009)

WISCONSIN BOARD OF VETERANS AFFAIRS
VETERAN LIFETIME ACHIEVEMENT AWARD

Ann and Jack enjoying one another's company

As a full-blooded Irishman, it was a special honor to be named "Irish Person of the Year" by the Dane County Shamrock Club in March 2010, and to participate in the Saint Patrick's Day ceremony at the State Capitol and in the parade that followed.

Program for the "Irish Person of the Year" ceremony.

Above: Middleton Mayor Kurt Sonnentag, Sheriff Dave Mahoney, and Jack.

In April 2010, as a WW II veteran, I was thrilled to participate in the Badger Honor Flight to Washington, D.C., which was truly a very memorable and emotional experience.

I was truly honored to be inducted into the Officer Candidate School Hall of Fame at Fort Benning, Georgia, with a very nice ceremony there on May 8th, 2017.

On November 9, 2017, Catholic Charities honored me with a Leadership Award for my many years of service to the church. The award was given at their annual "Faith in Action" awards celebration dinner.

MONDAY, JUNE 5, 2017

Elmira native John Rogan, right, is inducted into the Officer Candidate School Hall of Fame during a May 8 ceremony.

Military honor bestowed on World War II veteran

BUZZ ABOUT YOU
JEFF MURRAY

An Elmira native who served in the U.S. Army during the World War II era was recently honored in connection with his service.

John F. Rogan, 90, of Middleton, Wisconsin, was officially inducted into the Officer Candidate School Hall of Fame Class of 2017 on May 8 at the National Infantry Museum in Columbus, Georgia, home of Fort Benning.

Rogan was also recognized as a World War II veteran at the Patterson Award Banquet on May 9, also at the National Infantry Museum.

Rogan was the most senior member of his Hall of Fame Class of 2017, having been commissioned on Nov. 1, 1946 via the Army Finance School Officer Candidate School.

Rogan, who retired from the Army with the rank of colonel, graduated from St. Patrick's grade school and Elmira Catholic High School before enlisting in the Army and still has family members living in the Elmira area.

Jack Rogan receiving the Catholic Charities Leadership Award, presented by Michael Morey, Event Co-Chair (Nov. 9, 2017)

MEMORIAL DAY

A SPECIAL SUPPLEMENT
IN THE CATHOLIC HERALD,
DIOCESE OF MADISON

May 25, 2017

Colonel John F. Rogan inducted into Hall of Fame

BY MARY C. UHLER
Catholic Herald Staff

Usually Memorial Day is set aside as a holiday to remember people who died while serving in our country's armed forces.

However, it also seems to be an appropriate time to honor those who are still with us for their service to our country.

Hall of Fame

One of those persons recently selected is Colonel John F. "Jack" Rogan, United States Army, Retired.

He was recently selected for the Officer Candidate School (OCS) Hall of Fame Class of 2017. He was inducted in a ceremony held at the National Infantry Museum in Columbus, Ga.

The OCS Hall of Fame honors graduates of the federal Army Officer Candidate School who have distinguished themselves in military or civilian pursuits.

The Hall of Fame includes many notable and prestigious graduates, such as former Senator Bob Dole," said Major General Eric J. Wesley, U.S. Army Commanding General, in notifying Colonel Rogan of his selection.

He told Colonel Rogan, "Due to your exceptional dedication and service to your country, I am honored to congratulate you on your induction into this elite group."

Colonel Rogan was inducted into the OCS Hall of Fame with a unanimous vote.

Service experience

Born in 1926 in New York City, N.Y., and raised in Gortgarn, Northern Ireland, and Elmira, N.Y. Rogan attended St. Andrew Seminary in

He relinquished divinity school deferment to be drafted into the U.S. Army on June 29, 1945, for combat training at Camp Wheeler, Ga.

Following Japan's surrender, he transferred to the Finance Corps, graduated with honors from Officer Candidate School, and was commissioned a Second Lieutenant in the Army Finance Corps in November 1946.

Over the next 25 years, he served as a Finance Disbursing Officer with the Occupation Forces in Tokyo, Japan; an Artillery Battery Commander, Battalion Operations, and Training Officer with the 52nd Artillery Brigade at Fort Hancock,

See Colonel Rogan Page 2B

Colonel John F. "Jack" Rogan, United States Army retired, stands next to his profile as one of the Officer Candidate School Hall of Fame inductees at the National Infantry Museum in Columbus, Ga.

Family gathering at Bishop's Bay Country Club. From top: Mike, David, Sue, Vince, Kathy, Jack, Ann, Aidan (Maureen and Vince's son), Maureen, Cameron (Maureen and Vince's daughter), Kelsey (Patty and Jim's daughter), and Patty

Back row: Kelsey (Patty and Jim's daughter), Sue, Maureen, Cameron (Maureen and Vince's daughter), Judy (Jack's wife), and Mike. Front row: Patty, Ann, Jack, Jack Jr., and Trevor (Jack and Judy's son)

CHAPTER 16
ANN'S HEALTH DECLINES

In March 1997, Ann experienced chest pain while carrying groceries. She immediately called her doctor, but he did not think it was anything serious. It turned out to be a heart attack and Ann had to undergo triple bypass heart surgery. In May 1999, she was hospitalized for four days due to a mild heart attack from a blocked artery, followed by an outpatient cardiac rehabilitation program.

As the oldest sibling in her family, Ann witnessed the death of four of her siblings, twins Bob and Dick and sisters, Lucille and Patty, who both spent many years in facilities that care for individuals with Alzheimer's. Patty had early onset Alzheimer's and died at age 60. Naturally, Ann was very concerned that this could happen to her as well.

In the summer of 2007, I became aware that Ann was experiencing short-term memory problems, so I made an appointment with her doctor for a memory assessment. These tests proved to be very upsetting to Ann and she made me promise never to subject her to such assessments again. I felt terrible about the whole procedure and kept my promise to her. In subsequent years, she reached the point where she preferred to stay at home in familiar surroundings rather than attend various social and church-related events, which made her uncomfortable.

As her memory problems increased, along with some delusions/hallucinations at night, it was important for me to provide full-time care of Ann. I let the Bishop and others know that I needed to step down from various roles and responsibilities so I could be with Ann. I was afraid that she might fall down the stairs, inadvertently turn on the stove, or wander out the front door. I awakened immediately if she got up in the night and made sure she returned to bed safely.

In July 2010, we celebrated our 60th wedding anniversary with our family at Bishop's Bay Country Club. It was wonderful to enjoy dinner with all nine of our children and their spouses and children.

Jack and Ann's 60th anniversary celebration at Bishop's Bay Country Club in Madison (July 2010)

In San Diego (2013). Back row: Colleen, Krista (Colleen and Antonio's daughter), and Mike. Front row: Ann, Jack, Antonio (Colleen's husband), and Kyle (Colleen and Antonio's son)

*With the Dunne family in Port Laoise Ireland. From left: Elena
(Edward's wife), Emma, Paddy, Breege, Edward, Ann, Jack,
and Patty. (June 2013)*

*Ann and Jack at an old
Irish pub (June 2013)*

Celebrating Jack's 88th birthday (July 2014)

*Ann and Jack enjoying breakfast at a restaurant in
Middleton, Wisconsin (July 2014)*

Celebrating Ann's 90th birthday (September 2014)

Unfortunately, in October 2014, Ann did fall in the bathroom during the night, causing head, back, and foot injuries. She was taken by ambulance to the hospital and the doctors were concerned that she may have had a minor stroke.

Ann and I always got a flu vaccine in October and never had a problem until November 18, 2014, when we both came down with a bad case of the flu. When we were both in bed upstairs, I thought I heard the doorbell ring, but I was too dizzy to get up to answer the door. I told Ann not to try to answer the door either, but she may have forgotten. Unbeknownst to me, she went downstairs and, for some reason, stepped outside. She fell on the slippery sidewalk right in front of our house, causing a head injury and serious bleeding in her brain. Our son, Kevin, found her on the sidewalk and we rushed her to the emergency room.

The doctors informed us that it was too risky to attempt surgery to stop the bleeding in her brain. Besides, in her Power of Attorney for Health, Ann clearly stipulated to me as her designated representative that, in such a situation as this, she did not want any extra or special measures to be taken to prolong her life. Although the children and I tried to provide round-the-clock care for Ann in our home with "come in" hospice care, we needed qualified nursing staff to administer the proper pain shots that she needed. We moved her to Agrace hospice care in December, 2014.

Our children were very helpful during this difficult period. They flew in from around the country and took turns staying overnight with Ann at Agrace and supported me. Although I did not admit it to myself, caring for Ann took a toll on me. I developed diverticulitis, an infection, and was hospitalized during this time. I had to have four drainage tubes inserted in my abdomen, which needed to be drained and cleaned several times a day. My children took turns staying with me and assisting with my care.

Jack Jr. was at Agrace on January 28, 2015 when Ann passed away. Although I visited her daily and stay with her until nightfall, I regrettably decided to leave before dark to avoid driving on the highway because of my vision difficulties at night. As soon as I arrived at home, the phone rang. It was Jack saying that Ann had passed away at 6 p.m. Perhaps it was meant to be that way, but I wish I had been with her when she died.

We held Ann's funeral at St. Bernard's Catholic Church in Middleton on February 2, 2015 at noon, with a visitation at 10 a.m. prior to the Mass, a lunch after the service, and a private burial at Resurrection Cemetery. Several of our adult children were very helpful with the obituary, arranging for floral arrangements, setting up pictures of Ann in the church and Parish Center, and planning the luncheon menu. The photo of Ann in the obituary and in the Mass program was one that she and I really loved. I keep this photo next to my desk in my office. Ann's favorite color was blue, so we picked out a beautiful blue dress for her burial.

Despite the bitter cold day in early February, many people came to celebrate her life. We assumed that Monsignor Dushack, our Pastor at the time, would be the Celebrant for Ann's funeral Mass, but discovered that he was on vacation at the time. Father Bekala stepped in and did a very nice job. Monsignors Michael Burke and Daniel Ganshert, long-time friends, were co-celebrants, and Bishop Robert Morlino gave the final blessing. Previously, each of the priests had visited Ann at Agrace Hospice Care to pray for her and give their blessing. After the mass, we had a special meal in the parish hall. Ann is buried at Resurrection Cemetery, a diocesan cemetery in Madison.

By the way, Ann and I had made arrangements years ago for our funerals, including the type and color of our caskets. We had also selected our grave sites and kept notes on our funeral service preferences.

We were surprised to meet two individuals from the Red Cross at Ann's funeral service. They had read Ann's obituary and were amazed to learn about her story. They recommended that she receive a special Legacy Award from the National Headquarters of the American Red Cross in Washington for her outstanding service to our armed forces during World War II and Korea.

One of the women spent considerable time with me coming up with the recommendation for the award, which was presented to us at a special dinner gathering at our local Red Cross office in Madison on November 6, 2015. The event was attended by top representatives from the National Headquarters.

We were grateful to receive the award honoring Ann's service during two wars, but, regrettably, it came posthumously.

Certificate for Exemplary Service

Posthumous Recognition Of

Anna May Rogan

For dedicated service to the U.S. Armed Forces deployed in support of
combat operations in Japan and Korea during World War II
and the Korean War.

Your support of the American Red Cross Service to the Armed Forces
mission and your service under difficult circumstances is to be commended
and is hereby recognized with gratitude and respect.

Bonnie McElveen-Hunter
Chairman

Gail J. McGovern
President and CEO

Koby J. Langley
Senior Vice President
Service to the Armed Forces

November 6, 2015

American Red Cross

Although Ann did not actually serve in the military as such, she was granted special honorary membership in "Women In Military Service For America" in recognition and appreciation for her dedicated Red Cross service to our Armed Forces in Korea and Japan from 1948-1951. She remained an active member of this organization until her death in January 2015. Once they became aware of Ann's passing, they sent a very nice Certificate of Appreciation/Recognition and cover letter.

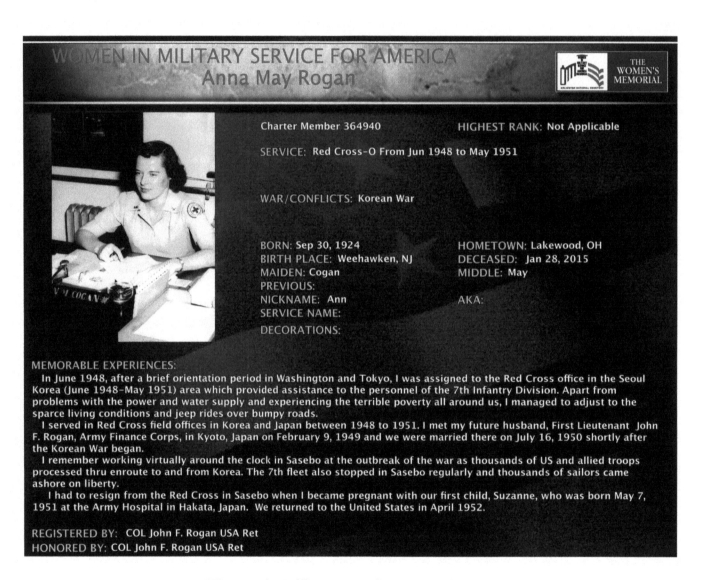

WOMEN IN MILITARY SERVICE FOR AMERICA
Anna May Rogan

THE WOMEN'S MEMORIAL

Charter Member 364940   HIGHEST RANK: Not Applicable

SERVICE: Red Cross-O From Jun 1948 to May 1951

WAR/CONFLICTS: Korean War

BORN: Sep 30, 1924   HOMETOWN: Lakewood, OH
BIRTH PLACE: Weehawken, NJ   DECEASED: Jan 28, 2015
MAIDEN: Cogan   MIDDLE: May
PREVIOUS:
NICKNAME: Ann   AKA:
SERVICE NAME:
DECORATIONS:

MEMORABLE EXPERIENCES:
   In June 1948, after a brief orientation period in Washington and Tokyo, I was assigned to the Red Cross office in the Seoul Korea (June 1948–May 1951) area which provided assistance to the personnel of the 7th Infantry Division. Apart from problems with the power and water supply and experiencing the terrible poverty all around us, I managed to adjust to the sparce living conditions and jeep rides over bumpy roads.
   I served in Red Cross field offices in Korea and Japan between 1948 to 1951. I met my future husband, First Lieutenant John F. Rogan, Army Finance Corps, in Kyoto, Japan on February 9, 1949 and we were married there on July 16, 1950 shortly after the Korean War began.
   I remember working virtually around the clock in Sasebo at the outbreak of the war as thousands of US and allied troops processed thru enroute to and from Korea. The 7th fleet also stopped in Sasebo regularly and thousands of sailors came ashore on liberty.
   I had to resign from the Red Cross in Sasebo when I became pregnant with our first child, Suzanne, who was born May 7, 1951 at the Army Hospital in Hakata, Japan. We returned to the United States in April 1952.

REGISTERED BY: COL John F. Rogan USA Ret
HONORED BY: COL John F. Rogan USA Ret

Women in Military Service recognition.

CHAPTER 17
IN LOVING MEMORY OF ANN

Ann often said that "Fate brought us together, but our Faith kept us together." She was so right! In the early years of my military career, I had occasions to travel by train from Indianapolis or St. Louis to Elmira, New York to visit my parents. I recall having to change trains in Cleveland, and having a good layover there before continuing to Buffalo and Elmira. To pass the time, I would enjoy a nice meal at a restaurant at or near the rail station and would also take a walk up to the main street. When I mentioned this to Ann after we met, she recalled often changing busses or the trolley there. I never imagined at the time that I would someday meet the love of my life from the Cleveland area.

Of course, we never would have met in Kyoto, Japan in February 1949 if Ann had not decided to join the American Red Cross as her contribution to the war effort, and wound up in Japan after a short stay in Korea. Also, we never would have met if I had decided against agreeing to an overseas special assignment in Japan, and had our bowling team not qualified for the Army Bowling Championship Tournament in Kyoto. Finally, we never would have met had not Ann's Red Cross friend at Camp Zama encouraged me to give Ann a call. The rest, as they say, is history.

In her younger days, Ann enjoyed tennis, swimming, biking, horseback riding, and dancing. She loved being at popular Cedar Point and riding the roller coasters. Before our children began to arrive, Ann and I took advantage of every opportunity to go dancing. Raising nine children prevented us from doing much dancing until they were older, but years later, we managed to attend a refresher dance program at the Officers' Club while at West Point and enjoyed dancing the familiar foxtrot, tango, rhumba, and a few of the newer dance numbers.

Once the children had left home, we enjoyed taking long walks together around the neighborhood and Pheasant Branch Creek trails through the woods. Sometimes she would walk with a friend if I was unavailable or she would listen to music on her Sony Walkman if she walked alone. We also enjoyed the shows at the Madison

Overture Center and Concerts on the Square, plus the Capitol City Band concerts in the nearby Hilldale Mall area.

We also enjoyed taking short drives to nearby towns to enjoy the beautiful scenery and would stop for lunch at a favorite spot. We also enjoyed taking longer trips after my retirement to visit our children, attend national conferences, or to visit potential retirement locations.

Ann was a very religious person in every sense of the word, and remained an active member of our parish. Her Catholic school upbringing was evident throughout her life.

Since I was so involved in work-related activities during my career, Ann was in charge of the household. She was tireless, loving, incredibly hard working, and selfless as she took care of the children, cleaning, shopping, laundry, and paying the bills. Her secretarial training and experience as the personal secretary to the President of the Sales Division at Standard Oil of Ohio came in very handy in keeping everything running smoothly.

Despite her very busy homemaker schedule, Ann somehow managed to keep in touch with friends and family members using her amazing typing and shorthand skills to full advantage. She remained in frequent touch with her friends from high school, as well as all of our relatives and military friends through annual Christmas letters. I've enjoyed reading copies of these letters now as I recall the wonderful times we had together as a family.

Ann's planning and organization skills were a huge asset during our various travels. We depended on her map-reading and general navigating skills. She did a remarkable job of compiling a notebook of all of the pertinent information about each trip, which I occasionally enjoy reviewing.

As covered previously in the book, we were blessed with nine beautiful children born around the world during various military assignments throughout the course of my 25-year active duty Army career. We are also blessed to have nine lovely grandchildren.

During the years after my retirement in August 1983, Ann and I enjoyed spending the month of January in San Diego, staying at the Miramar Marine Corps Air Base, as our annual winter escape until it became too much for her health-wise. Now our children accompany me to San Diego in January.

Celebrating Jack's 90th birthday at our family home in Middleton, WI.
Front row: Kathy, Maureen, Jack, Patty, Judy (Jack Jr.'s wife), Kelsey (Patty and Jim's daughter), and Jenna (Jack and Judy's daughter).
Back row: Jack Jr., Vince (Maureen's husband), Mike, Ryan (Patty and Jim's son), Kevin, Jim (Patty's husband), and Jenna's boyfriend.

Visiting with Madison bishop and priests while vacationing in San Diego

Family in Colorado for Jack and Judy's wedding.
From left: David, Patty, Mike, Kathy, Maureen, Kevin, Ann, Colleen, and Jack

I thank God every day for bringing us together and blessing our marriage of 64+ wonderful years together. Ann and I always remembered each other's birthdays and our anniversary by selecting just the right card for each other and writing a personal note. When she passed away, I discovered that she had kept every one of the cards that I gave her, as I had done with the cards from her. Now, as each important event in our lives approaches, I pull out the cards we had sent to each other at the time and find that to be helpful in dealing with her death and loneliness. She did so much to support my career, especially during the periods of separation. She was one special gal—so beautiful in every way.

This book is intended as a special tribute to my lovely wife and dedicated in her honor, memory, and legacy. She was a very special mother and grandmother who is always in my thoughts and prayers. I know she is in Heaven because of her faith-filled life and I am thankful that she does not have to worry anymore about the advanced stages of Alzheimer's. I feel her presence around me all the time, which is comforting during this very difficult and lonely phase of my life, and find solace in the conversations that I have with her throughout the day. I am praying for the day when, God willing, we will be back together in Heaven for all eternity.

THE NINE GRANDCHILDREN

Ann and Jack with their first grandchildren, Trevor (born 1984) and Jenna (born 1987). In front: Ann and Trevor. In rear: David, Jack, Judy (Jack's wife), Jack Jr., Kathy, and Jenna

Gathering at the family home in Middleton. From left: Vince Cozzi, David Rogan, baby Jenna, Maureen Rogan, Michael Rogan, Sue Rogan (Mike's wife), Colleen Rogan. In front: Trevor Rogan, Judy Rogan (Jack Jr.'s wife), and Kathy Rogan

*Ann and Jack with their 3rd grandchild, Ryan Rogan
Padgham in Syracuse, NY (1990)*

*From left: Granddaughter Julie (Mike and Sue's daughter) with Mike (holding baby
Kelsey, born 1993), Ann, Colleen, and Jack*

Patty with Ryan and Kelsey (grandchildren #3 and #4)

Ann with daughter Maureen and grandson Aidan (1998)

Jack and Ann with daughter Colleen and grandson, Kyle (1998)

*Ann and Jack with granddaughter, Cameron (Maureen and
Vince's daughter) (2001)*

Front row: Grandchildren Kyle, Cameron, and Krista, Ann, granddaughter Kelsey, and Kathy. Back row: Patty, Jack, Colleen, Jack Jr., Mike, Kevin, Sue, and Maureen (Bishops Bay Country Club, 2010)

CPSIA information can be obtained
at www.ICGtesting.com
Printed in the USA
BVHW020732090719

552921BV00005BA/37/P